FRANCE

LA DOUCEUR DE VIVRE

WHITE STAR PUBLISHERS

Text
Simonetta Crescimbene

Graphic design
Patrizia Balocco

Contents

1 *The origins of the landscaped garden, one of France's many famous legacies to the world, lie in the creations of André le Nôtre (1613-1700), the genial landscape architect whose most famous works are the gardens of Versailles.*

2-3 *Orderly rows of grape vines stretch along the hillsides of Alsace, near Riquewihr. In the fall, these villages are the setting for festivals and celebrations.*

4-5 *Slate roofs stretch as far as the eye can see in the broad valley carved by the Seine in ancient times: it is the "nest" of Paris, just under 35 sq. miles (90 sq. km) that contain the wonders and subtleties of this city cherished by the world. In the photo, Île de la Cité is dominated by the cathedral of Notre-Dame, easily seen on the right. On the island, the other spire that stands out for its height belongs to Sainte-Chapelle, flanked on the left by the Conciergerie, which was part of the royal palace until the 14th century and later became the courthouse and notorious prison.*

6 *Sainte-Chapelle was built as a shrine in which to store a relic believed to be Christ's crown of thorns, and other relics now kept in the Treasury of Notre-Dame. The upper chapel – there are two, one set atop the other – is almost entirely made of windows, in a spectacular example of architectural precision.*

7 *Notre-Dame, a masterpiece of Gothic architecture, built between 1163 and 1250, underwent further modifications in later centuries. Today, visitors can roam the setting of the adventures of Quasimodo, the hunchback, and Esmeralda, as described by Victor Hugo, or improvise a merry outing among grotesques and gargoyles, as restored by the architect Viollet-le-Duc.*

8-9 *A wide avenue lined with plane trees leads to the bridge at the entrance to the château of Chenonceaux, surrounded by French gardens enclosed by a moat. At the rear, a long five-arch bridge topped by a gallery crosses the River Cher. In the 16th century it was a setting for fêtes and banquets held by the court of Catherine de' Medici.*

© 2006 White Star S.p.A.
New updated edition

© 1993 White Star S.p.A.
Via C. Sassone, 22/24
13100 Vercelli, Italy
www.whitestar.it

ISBN 88-544-0115-3

Reprints:
1 2 3 4 5 6   10 09 08 07 06

Color separation by Magenta Lit. Con., Singapore
Printed in Singapore

10 *In a harsh environment, softened here and there only by the red tiled roofs of the villas and the sparse Mediterranean vegetation, a calcareous spur stretches out toward a sea so blue that it leaves no doubts: this is the Côte d'Azur in the vicinity of Marseille, in the area with the rocky formations known as Calanques, a paradise for rock-climbers and hikers. The highly unique conformation of the territory, bristling with rocky needles and furrowed by deep trenches, creates a variety of amazing scenic settings.*

10-11 *The geological eras reveal their clear sedimentary "registers" along the Falaise d'Aval, in the département of Seine-Maritime, not far from Le Havre. France's northern coastline recalls, in more than one stretch, the shores on the other side of the English Channel, from which it was separated in ancient times by the movement of the earth's crust.*

Introduction

Mirabeau, Fontenay-aux-Roses, Rochefort, Fleurance, Les Sables-d'Olonne, Pont Saint-Esprit... just the sound of French place names is sufficient to evoke images of still lakes, lush gardens, and fairy-tale cottages. Modern readers, however, may be more familiar with terms to describe environmental catastrophe, unscrupulous development, and rogue industrialization. We are almost reluctant to believe that a even wise government can any longer protect the pastoral beauty of the French countryside.

And so, as a visitor crosses the French border, there is a considerable temptation to wander at large, to eliminate, somehow, distances and obstacles; in brief, to take in at one glance the whole of the nation – the shimmering chalk cliffs of Étretat, the geological curiosities of the Puys mountains, the vast scented fields of lavender and rosemary in the Garrigues – so that no single wonder or marvel can elude one's gaze. Before the infinite variety of France, the visitor is disarmed. It is hard to say which is more overwhelming: the abundance and loveliness of the landscape, or the wealth of the past. From the Midi to the North, history seems to leap out from every corner. Spanning the Paleolithic to the contemporary era, it postures and declaims – in the form of urban graffiti or dashing Impressionist brushstrokes, Gothic spires or modern cantilevers, the cave paintings of Lascaux or the 485-ft (148 m) Tour EDF at La Défense, completed in 2002.

It is perhaps no accident that we have borrowed the term *avant-garde*. Throughout history, in every circumstance and juncture, the French have broken the chains of tradition and given free rein to innovation and creativity; they have done so in settings that range from the chilly garrets of the Bohemians to the monumental splendor described in French as *la grandeur*. In the student revolts of May 1968, *L'imagination au pouvoir* (roughly, "power to the imagination") was a slogan chanted outside the Sorbonne; in a sense, however, it is a venerable motif of French culture.

Intuitive leaps can be just as important in technological progress as the most painstaking calculations. The visionary genius of Jules Verne

provides an adequate demonstration of this adage, as does the pioneering photography and cinematography of Jacques Daguerre and the Frères Lumière, who triggered a revolution in modern culture by broadening the horizons of artistic media. And nowadays, the films of René Clair, Jean Cocteau, Claude Chabrol, François Truffaut, Louis Malle and Jean-Luc Godard occupy an honored place in the annals of cinema; they communicate to the rest of the world an authentic flavor of French spirit. That *esprit* – or spirit – has a special meaning to a great many people; it evokes France, but it also evokes a period of their lives. It summons up memories of bitter-voiced poets, philosophers and café singers, denouncing the nausea and ennui of modern life. It recalls the existential travail of an entire generation of European intellectuals. Yet it also evokes the rustle of silk and chiffon, luxurious fashion shows in vintage newsreels and the first glimmerings of the hedonistic age of Haute Couture. France is, in short, a hotbed of new ideas; often the French succeed in turning these ideas into "trends" that sweep the world.

This nation, ever youthful and new, possesses a remarkable equilibrium, a fine balance between daring and tradition, between the spectacular and the understated. There is a solid and versatile culture tucked away in the heart of each region. Part of the challenge – and joy – of touring France is to discover these separate traditions. An imaginative visitor, for instance, may choose to spend time drifting along the placid canals of Burgundy. This canal network, built centuries ago, is the best known one in France, but form Normandy to Provence, there are numerous other wonderful river and canal routes, navigable by barge. The barges, or *péniches*, ply the rivers at a steady five knots, trailing streams of wavelets and ripples. At this leisurely pace, the passengers can enjoy the verdant landscape as it creeps by, reflected in the mirroring water. In the succession of locks, these waterways link the most important rivers in France – the Seine, the Loire, the Rhône and the Saône become paths along which one can set out to explore the homeland of the ancient Gauls, here and there unchanged through millennia of history. And, if the charms of nature are not sufficient to soothe the soul, there are the charms of French dining.

Entrancing riverfront villages with evocative names welcome the amateur sailor; here one can dock directly at restaurants serving such local specialties as *poulet flambé à la moutarde* or *pain d'épice dijonnais*, liberally accompanied by a fine dry Chablis or a white Mâcon. The Côte d'Or possesses two wine-growing regions: the Côte de Nuits in the north and the Côte de Beaune in the south. In this area, during the summer, both locals and well-informed visitors stroll along the illuminated rows of the vineyards and vintners' traditional *caves* dot the landscape, amidst a profusion of colorful gardens and delicate pergolas, stately bell towers and medieval villages, and cool groves of plane and chestnut trees. Everywhere one sees evidence of the loving pride of the residents. Perhaps the most fitting representative of this region is the *éclusier*, or lock-keeper, who courteously ushers the barge through the hydraulic machinery of the locks with the same traditional motions and gestures used by his fathers and his grandfathers before him. While waiting for the barge to rise or settle to the level of a stream ahead, a visitor should take advantage of the lock-keeper's lore. He may describe some of the remarkable architectural and historical treasures of the region, often overlooked by travelers.

Among the monuments those travelers overlook are no fewer than 350 Romanesque churches. Cluny, with its renowned Benedictine abbey, was the cornerstone of the Burgundian Romanesque school of building, a style that spread over all of Europe. All over the region, small towns and villages still possess vestiges of this great architectural revolution. The countryside abounds, therefore, in fairy-tale landscapes, spellbinding at times; one can sense the excitement of artistic innovation that must have swept this region ten centuries before, without ever having to leave the comfort of the barge, with its comfortable deck and the gentle sway of the *maison*, or cabin. This is French living at its most carefree.

This charmed union between earth and water may serve as a fitting prologue to another, equally bewitching region: Brittany. Here, in bracing contrast with the quiet, enameled waters of Burgundy, rough Atlantic waves crush foaming onto the red granite rocks of the northern coast or the Breton peninsula. This last strip of land, stretching out into the mighty ocean, is called Finistère, a name taken from the Latin *finis terrae*, which means "end of the land." On this stark backdrop, nature rages; here, pirates once roamed the coasts, looting and laying waste on shore and at sea. Now brigantines and galleons have been replaced by fishing boats, hull down on the horizon under a changing, lowering sky. The tangy and pungent aroma of the waves hovers over shoals, reefs and islets, which disappear and resurface with the cadenced surge of the tides.

Over millennia, the waves have painstakingly carved away at the rocky shores, studded with seashells and crabs. The intricate coastline is a perfect vantage point from which to observe the ocean, in all its timeless mystery.

The ebb and flow of the water is a perfect corollary to the lives led here. This tenacious, stubborn people, with a language and a past perhaps more closely linked to Britain than to a continental France, seems to have modeled itself on the sea. The Bretons are ocean-farers, deeply marked by the awareness of life's fragility in the face of stern nature. They are proud of all they have survived; after waves of invaders – first Roman armies, and then Celtic and Frankish settlers – Brittany became an independent dukedom, a status it defended until the inevitable surrender to growing French might in 1532. Despite the loss of political independence, the region remained culturally and artistically distinct, and some folkways are intact today. In small towns it is not rare to see knots of matrons commenting, in Breton dialect, on the Sunday sermon, their hair adorned with the intricate and traditional lace headgear. These spotless white folds of lace are worn on the numerous religious and town feast-days, such as the blessing of the fishing nets, which takes place in Concarneau in the month of August.

From May to September, during the so-called *pardons*, the visitor has the best opportunity, however, to explore the Breton spirit, which imbues the largest towns as profoundly as it does the most remote village. These processions are the latter-day version of feasts held to honor the Virgin and all of the saints; the Church once granted plenary indulgence to all the faithful on those occasions. A deep-seated mysticism and austere customs are – and were, in Celtic tradition – traits that links Armor, the maritime section of Brittany, with Argoat, the inland region, countrified and heavily wooded. The distinctive *enclos paroissiaux*, or walled squares surrounding the church, and the unsettling figures of the *calvaries*, gazing out at us across centuries of medieval gloom, are eloquent of an ancient spirituality. Ossuaries, cemeteries, chapels and fountains have been monuments of Christian inspiration through the centuries, but one of the most peculiar monuments in Brittany is equally religious – the megaliths of Carnac. One's first impression upon entering the plain of Ménec is that of being overwhelmed by the thousands of colossal upright stones, standing in circular or rectangular array or, here and there, in solitary majesty. It is believed that these stones were erected by sun-worshiping peoples who dwelt here in the third and second millennia B.C. These gigantic primitive temples stand witness to the unimaginable efforts these peoples were willing to lavish in order to exalt the glory of their god. The

12-13 The Côte d'Or is the wide area in Burgundy where excellent wines such as Beaujolais and Chablis are produced. It is divided into two areas: the Côte de Nuits in the North, famous for the red wines of Nuits St. Georges, Chambolle-Musigny, Morey St. Denis, and the Côte de Beaune, where such white and red wines as Pommard, Auxey-Duresses, St.-Romain, and Volnay are produced.

14-15 A golden field of sunflowers, seemingly boundless in this pictures, shows the inspiring Provençal landscape, which Van Gogh reproduced majestically during his stay at Arles.

16 top These proud pines and stand in the national of Ecrins, located in the Dauphiné. The park's highest points are Mont Pelvoux and the Barre des Écrins; in this remarkable protected area one can hike, climb, or cycle.

16 bottom La Vallouise, a river valley carved out by the Durance, is a pleasant route to Briançon. Equidistant from the national park of Écrins and the wilderness of the Queyras, this is a perfect staging area for a number of hikes.

17 The Atlantic Pyrenees slope gently down to the ocean. The steady sunlight from May on makes trekking from one high valley to another particularly enjoyable.

19 As if it were suspended in an exclusive, tiny world that changes according to the tides, Mont-Saint-Michel offers visitors unique, thrilling, and spiritual experiences. The vastness of the environment only enhances the uniqueness of this abbey/hamlet born upon granite, a refuge for bodies and souls built with dogged determination between the 7th and 15th centuries.

sight of these stones at sunset, their long shadows creeping across the earth, is impressive and memorable. Menhirs, dolmens, châteaux and chapels – all are built of the same hard gray granite, as if every single thing had petrified at the dawn of creation. Inland, the lush green of the forest is broken at intervals by the deep blue of the canals, mirroring the solid granite houses with their sharply pitched blue-gray stone roofs.

This enchanting landscape, dotted with venerable mills, can be seen in the paintings of the artists of Pont-Aven, chief among them Paul Gauguin. It is scarcely surprising that these artists should have given up Paris, seeking inspiration amidst the poetic nature of Brittany. The region attracted writers as well as painters – Guy de Maupassant and Guillaume Apollinaire lived here. Again, little wonder, considering Brittany's ancient literary tradition – this is the setting for the medieval legends of King Arthur. In the so-called Dark Ages, the forest of Brocéliande extended across the Breton heartland, offering imaginary haven to such fabled characters as Lancelot and the sorcerer Merlin.

The year 1000, which marked the dawn of a new millennium, was the turning point in what is now France. In just three centuries, dozens of cathedrals and hundreds of churches sprang up across the land. In those days, everyone lent a hand in the construction of religious buildings – some offered manual labor, so as to atone for past sins with the sweat of their brows; others offered funds in exchange for dispensations. It was through the latter system of exchange that the town of Rouen, in Normandy, obtained a flamboyant Gothic masterpiece, La Tour de Beurre, or the Butter Tower. This remarkable construction was financed by the townspeople in exchange for ecclesiastic authorization to eat butter during Lent. Whatever the circumstances, however, the profusion of new churches and cathedrals was an expression of a great and widely felt passion. Medieval mysticism launched the imaginations of builders and architects upward, in a heaven-bent crescendo of aspiration that took the form of tapering arches, Gothic vaults, flying buttresses and towering spires and pinnacles. Towers and belfries attained dizzying heights; stone was rendered light and airy by oculi, fretwork, and rose windows as intricate as the finest lace. Parti-colored stained-glass windows brought shafts of light through the massive walls, while statues of saints, devils and grotesque monsters adorned the exterior. These buildings sprang up across all of what is now France, but they were especially numerous in Île-de-France and Normandy.

Normandy, in particular, boasts the churches and cathedrals of Evreux, Rouen, Fécamp, Lisieux, Caen, Bayeux, Coutances and Mont-Saint-Michel; the latter abbey stands on the border with Brittany, and in some sense links the two regions. Nature and history have conspired to make Mont-Saint-Michel unlike anything else on earth – set amid an expanse of ever-changing sands which are illuminated by the restless coastal light and flooded at regular intervals by the most powerful tides in Europe, the island-abbey rears up, a startling metaphor for medieval society. Tourists flock to this portion of the Norman coastline, and many take the opportunity for a stroll across the tidal sands, enjoying some of the most spectacular views of the mount. Before doing so, however, it is wise to know just when the next high tide is expected. The waters rise rapidly, driving up the level of rivers and surrounding and engulfing the sandy shoals.

Normandy abounds in vernacular architecture; the *maison à colombage*, or dovecote, is particularly typical of the old section of Rouen. This style of construction varied freely from the Middle Ages to the Renaissance; the houses are, in turn, distinguished by sharp angles, straight lines or steep pitches; squat or soaring, ostentatious or understated; with wooden half-beams that mark their façades. Gustave Flaubert was originally from Normandy, and these houses serve as backdrops in many of his novels, including *Madame Bovary*.

Normandy's splendid Gothic stained glass, meant to elevate the spirit in mystical ecstasy, and Flaubert's remarkable writings, designed to revolutionize the novel, must share pride of place with yet another of the region's happy inventions, perhaps less noble, but equally vital to life here – Norman cider. The region is covered with vast orchards in which no fewer than seventy different varieties of apple tree flower each May, overwhelming the visitor with color and aroma. And in October, when the rest of France is busy harvesting grapes, the apple trees of Normandy are bowed down with ripe fruit. This is the time to visit the cider "vintners," to taste the aromatic fruit juice. Some of this juice, each year, will be distilled into the lively local eau-de-vie, Calvados.

Normandy reaped another, less joyful harvest during the massive Allied invasion in June of 1944, and the damage done by bombardment and shelling can still be seen here and there, and there are vast cemeteries where soldiers of all nationalities rest in eternity. And even these fields of stone and greensward can become tourist attractions, particularly if a well-known name appears on a headstone.

Likewise, the Parisian cemeteries of Père Lachaise, Montmartre, and Montparnasse are pleasant spots in which to stroll, along lanes crowded with marble angels, stone muses, and Baroque curlicues, dangling in silence. Paul Valéry, in his poem "Cimetière marin," based on the graveyard of Sète, wrote, "... La vie est vaste, étant ivre d'absence," roughly, "Life is vast here, drunk with absence...." And the tourists and visitors come in great numbers to pay their respects to a wide range of "absent" celebrities, such as Jim Morrison, Hector Berlioz, Chopin, Sarah Bernhardt, François Truffaut, Honoré de Balzac, and Jean-Paul Sartre, all of whom are joined at last in eternity.

Which brings us to the Île-de-France, heart of the nation, favored by nature and by history. The countryside is fertile and residents can stroll or hike through magnificent forests, like that of Fontainebleau. Here too, Gothic cathedrals and splendid châteaux dot the landscape. But the pride of Île-de-France is certainly Paris and her greater metropolitan area. The statistics of the French census tell us that one in every five Frenchmen is Parisian by birth or by residence. And the city's population continues to grow, burgeoning with new arrivals from all over France and from the rest of the world. Few of those who arrive in Paris, nowadays, come in search of artistic fame. Things were quite different at the turn of the 20th century – then Paris lured countless young men and women questing after glory, bartering drawings and finished paintings for canvas, paint, and a bottle of absinthe, according to the Bohemian legend. Pablo Picasso, Modigliani, Utrillo, and Léger lived in this picturesque Paris between the world wars. Still other young artists, their names long forgotten, experienced the same privations and endured the same poverty, but never savored the heady wine of fame and wealth.

Though not all Parisians are starving artists or penniless poets, there were times when Paris suffered great poverty; 19th-century novelists Emile Zola and Victor Hugo describe a city of widespread hunger and misery. Even amid severe want, Parisians have always worked hard to enjoy themselves, lavishing imagination and creativity on the pursuit of good times. Drawings and canvases by Degas and Toulouse-Lautrec depict the cheerful atmosphere of the *cafés-concerts* and country dances of the Belle Époque. Nowadays, too, the French and foreign tourists can still enjoy the city's charm, strolling idly through the narrow streets of the Marais, sitting down to a drink in a *café-théâtre* in the French quarter while listening to a French comic or a jazz band, lolling at a *terrasse*

along the Boulevard Saint-Germain, or promenading through the Luxembourg Gardens. Even though Paris works hard to keep the straight and serious face of a cultural and professional capital, she sets aside her most beautiful crannies and corners for sweet laziness! There are so many faces of Paris; tourists may amble off of the Lido or to the Crazy Horse Saloon, to admire the marmoreal beauty of the dancers. Hints of the Parisian gaiety celebrated by Edith Piaf can still be found along the banks of the Seine. The rows of green bookstalls attract crowds of amateur browsers and serious collectors, who stand enthralled by a first edition, an old engraving, a sepia photograph or a tattered postcard, complete with address, message and postmarked stamp; nearby, in Place Saint-Michel, comics and musicians attract crowds: Paris maintains her reputation – often amplified and exaggerated by the media – for elegant rendez-vous at the racetracks of Auteuil or Longchamp, for impressive official ceremonies on the Champs-Elysées, for spectacular haute-couture fashion shows or for the showings of artists in Place du Tertre. This is the flashy, traditional Paris of the postcards.

The real charm of Paris lies elsewhere however. It can be found in the heart of an old neighborhood, the intimate elegance of a gesture, the tireless labor of craftsmen and artisans: the silent work of cabinet makers in the Marais, the ceaseless shuffling patter of silk ballet slippers rehearsing *pas des deux* and *arabesques* at the Opéra, the lush and almost enchanted gardens tucked away behind the sober façades of *hôtels particuliers*, the stores with antique signboards, the vendors in the vast and sprawling flea markets – these are just a few of the hidden and often-overlooked faces of this infinitely fascinating city. With patience and dedication, each of every visitor can discover this secret garden in the heart of Paris.

The Île-de-France is not limited to Paris. The capital is surrounded by a constellation of châteaux, each of them unique and charming. To name just a few, Fontainbleau, Vaux-le-Vicomte, Versailles, each of which possesses a sumptuous garden designed by André Le Nôtre (1613-1700). These châteaux are architectural treasures in their own right; there are, moreover, brimful of magnificent masterpieces.

The true cornucopia of spectacular châteaux, however, is Touraine and the central stretch of the Loire river valley. If Burgundy is the heart of French Romanesque, and Normandy is unrivaled for its Gothic spires and flying buttresses, this fertile valley has shown the world the epitome of Renaissance style. Amboise, Chambord, Chenonceaux, Azay-le-Rideau, Blois, Chinon... each of these names corresponds to a

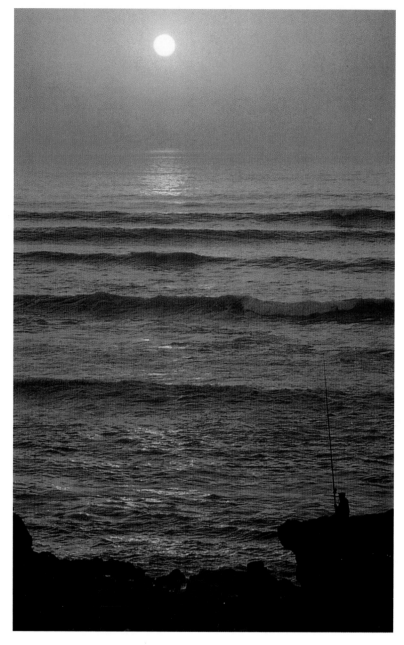

20 *These gently rolling waves at sunset, along the Basque coastline, are unusually peaceful. Usually, the waves break with violence, and surfers zigzag merrily across the foamy mountains of water.*

21 top *The port of the small seaside resort of Cancale enjoys a particularly privileged view, looking out as it does on the bay of Mont-Saint-Michel and the marshlands of Dol. Located just a few miles from the fortified village of Saint-Malo, this is a must for tourists who wish to see the real Brittany.*

21 center and bottom *Certain unspoiled stretches of the Breton coastline evoke the time when the Celts named this region "Armor," or "Land of the Sea." The ancient legends of this area still tinge it with a haunted air of mystery.*

22-23 *Soft pastels like watercolors tint the Burgundian countryside, among low rows of grapevines and fruit trees pruned like works of art. Wine is at the origin of the present-day fame of this historic French region, which also boasts a glorious history filled with participants like the Merovingian, Carolingian, and Frankish kingdoms, and later one of the most renowned duchies in the history of France and Europe from the Middle Ages to modern times. Close to the geographical heart of the French "hexagon," Burgundy also offers bewitching landscapes, featuring neatly organized farmland and less populated areas left to nature.*

château, where visitors can follow expert guides or learn from scholarly conservators; during the summer, they can enjoy the sound-and-light shows – *spectacles son et lumière.*

French poets have described the nation's rivers as routes for the conveyance of ideas as well as of freight. This poetic conceit was meant to underscore the venerable role, eminently solid after centuries of history, that the rivers of France continue to play in the life of the nation. Each region is organized around its chief river, and it is the leisurely flow of the river that sets the pace of life and change in small towns and villages. The Canal de la Marne au Rhin and the Canal du Rhône au Rhin join up with the Rhine in Strasbourg, on the Alsatian border, bone of contention and first victim in both world wars. In an irony of history, Strasbourg has now been declared the capital of Europe. Since 1982, the European parliament has held regular sessions here; when the parliament is sitting, the town is swept by unfamiliar bustle and activity. During the rest of the year, it remains a town of exquisitely provincial charm, with handsome half-beamed houses.

The wines of Alsace – Riesling, Tokay, and Sylvaner – enjoy excellent reputations, and are the product of a great tradition in the vintner's art. The orderly rows of the vineyards contrast sharply with the unruly exuberance of the century-old chestnuts, the beech trees, and the spruce pines; the trees become thicker in a riot of foliage as one enters the great Vosges forest. The traditional wine fairs offer an opportunity to show off the picturesque regional outfits, as are the folk festivals which reach some sort of Dionysian crescendo in the first week of September, when the wine spurts from the village fountain. In Colmar, a huge festival takes place in late August; the women dress in traditional garb and join the vintners to savor the succulent *choucroutes* (sauerkraut) and to sample the excellent Tokay.

Now let us leave Alsace and move on to Champagne. On the banks of the Seine, the town of Troyes boasts an amazing profusion of religious masterpieces in Gothic and Renaissance style. It is the Champagne, however, and not the artworks, that has made the place famous. It is said that a certain Dom Pérignon, a monk and the master of the wine cellars at the Abbey of Hautvillers in the late 17th century, was the inventor of what we now call Champagne, but it was not until the following century that Champagne acquired its official titles of nobility.

Along the banks of the Marne, one can stumble upon sanctuaries of Champagne, one after

another: Taittinger, Pommery, Lanson, Veuve Cliquot, Ruinart, and Piper-Heidsieck, and their vineyards, set off by granite markers or else enclosed behind walls. The geometric order of the vines sheers off and overlaps, mingling colors as in an Impressionist painting. This bright, sunny image, however, contrasts with the dark, subterranean world, branching off into thousands of ancient tunnels; here 600 million bottles are stored, lovingly guarded and protected from light and noise. If they were lined up, these tunnels in Reims and Épernay would stretch for nearly 200 miles. Great care and devotion are lavished, without regard for cost, in the maintenance of these stone treasure houses where, at a constant temperature (between 8° and 12° Centigrade), the wines of Champagne gradually acquire all of their highly prized qualities. Much like in Alsace, this kingdom of vineyards, with its impeccable rows of trellises, contrasts sharply with the anarchy of the luxuriant forest. Grape stalks and tendrils give way to oaks, spruce trees, and beeches in the national Parc de la Montagne of Reims, one of France's one hundred fifty-six national wildlife preserves. Visitors can enjoy guided "photo-safaris," rock-climbing, skiing, hiking, and exploring in the numerous caves and grottoes, featuring amazing limestone formations. In southern France, the emerald-green triangle between the Vézère and the Dordogne river valleys is dotted with twenty-five grottoes, inhabited in prehistoric times, and with thousands of relics that speak of the presence of humans since the dawn of time. In particular, this is where the skeleton of Cro-Magnon man was unearthed, an early specimen of *homo sapiens* who walked 30,000 years ago. The best-known sites are Les Eyzies, La Madeleine and, of course, the caves of Lascaux, where the earliest European humans painted astonishing works of cave art.

The French mountain chains, chief among them the Alps, the Pyrenees, and the Jura, are much frequented by nature lovers and by skiers. The winter sports complexes are extremely modern and boast thousands of chairlifts, skilifts, and funiculars, and – here and there – "ecomuseums" which provide information on the mountain paths.

Every region in France possesses its own unique features. To get to know them, one must leave the cities and towns and plunge into the countryside. An exploration of the most recondite corners of Provence, for instance, could begin in the East, where the torrential waters of the Verdon tumble through rocky gorges, or else floating down the waters of the Rhône to the delta, which spreads out through the marshlands of the Camargue. There, one finds a remarkable array of fauna: beavers and badgers, but also herons and pink flamingoes, wild ducks, teals, woodcocks, aigrettes, and others. There are wild white horses and savage black bulls. The landscape of reeds and wild rose is dotted, here and there, by small whitewashed cottages, with straw roofs and huge stables – *les cabanes*. These peaceful houses glitter in the sunlight, reflecting a distinctly Provençal light that appears in the work of some of the great artists of the past century – Matisse, Dufy, Gauguin, Cézanne, Picasso, Kandinsky... The people of Provence have fine-honed features, a clear mark of the hard labor involved in farming and herding. In Saint-Martin-de-la-Crau, a folk tradition still survives, involving the *gardians*, local cowboys, and vast herds of sheep; there is a festival on the day that the *gardians* take leave of the village and set off for the high pastures. Scarves and felt hats are proudly shown off, as they have been for centuries, during the religious service in which man and beast receive benediction; the festival reaches a climax when the herds of sheep, hesitantly bleating, are driven off through the narrow and intricate lanes of the village and up to the hills.

On the 24th and 25th of May, the town of Saintes-Maries-de-la-Mer comes to life as a remarkable group of individuals descend upon it. There are Gitanos, Zingari, Gitanes, Sintoes, Rom, Hungarian Gypsies, Adels, and Manouches, and they come from all over to worship, with pagan and Christian rites, the arrival in this region of Saintes Marie, Marie Jacobé, Marie Salomé, and Sarah-la-Kali, who was their servant, who arrived in the region around the first century A.D., according to legend. Today, the "Pilgrims of moonlight," as they are known, dance to the skittish rhythm of flamenco for two days without a break, and sing, in hoarse and mournful voices, around a bonfire. They end the celebration by solemnly walking in procession to the sea, where the "Three Maries" supposedly disembarked, in flight from persecution in Jerusalem. Provence differs from other regions both in terms of language and history. The *langue d'Oc*, the original language of Provence, has been supplanted by the *langue d'oïl*, imposed by Paris, but the Provençal dialect is still spoken. In historical terms, Provence differs sharply from the rest of France as well. Inthe 1st century B.C., Provence was the only Roman province in Gallic territory, and therefore it boasts many vestiges of Roman civilization.

In Orange, one can admire the splendid triumphal arch built by Julius Caesar and the perfectly preserved Roman theater, which contains an imposing statue of Augustus, 16 ft (4.8 m) high. Here, as in the

24-25 At the Rhône delta, where the river's twin streams meet the sea, there stretches a wild land, odorous with tamarisks, abounding in extraordinary flora (salicorne, saladelle) and fauna (beavers, herons, pink flamingoes, aigrettes, wild ducks...). Here too one finds white horses and black bulls, tall rushes and colorful wild roses, plentiful fishing and salt marshes. There is another, agrarian Camargue, a region of vast landholdings, sheep herding, vineyards, legumes, forage, and rice.

26-27 *The little Corsican town of Saint-Florent lies at the end of a gulf, on the north of the island, surrounded by groves of olive trees with twisted shapes, orderly vineyards, and fruit orchards, typical of the region. One can stroll and pass the time of day here very agreeably, along the marina and through the old town, clustered around the church, under the sheltering walls of the ancient Genoese citadel.*

arena in nearby Arles, these ancient theaters host performances of modern times, whether it be opera or bloody bullfights. The birth of civilization in this region dates back even further, to circa 600 B.C., when Greeks from Asia Minor founded Marseille and discovered the beauty of such coastal sites as Nice, Antibes and Cannes. Successive cultures left marks of their glory on this land troubled by the *mistral*, the rough north wind: in the white ruins of Glanum, in the Avignon of the pontiffs and in fortified inland villages. Craftsmanship vaunts a very ancient tradition, as in the manufacture of the *santons* (small clay Nativity figures) of Provence, or the pottery of Vallauris, already well known during the reign of the Roman emperor Tiberius – these ceramic creations enjoyed new popularity thanks to the innovative Picasso.

In the 16th century, in Grasse, Catherine de' Medici encouraged the distillation of fragrant perfumes and essences, today an important category in the French economy and a fundamental feature of French charm. Visitors to this remarkable land will find their needs cared for by a sophisticated industry of hospitality and by the natural generosity of the people. Artists in search of solitude and concentration have rediscovered the long-forgotten mountain villages, often called "eagles' nests." These delightful hideouts are not targeted by mass tourism, because they are so hard to reach, although they are often close to the coast. South of Marseille, "calanques," steep and jagged inlets, provide natural harbors for pleasure boats.

The international jet set may prevail on the Promenade des Anglais in Nice or along La Croisette in Cannes; the Basque coast, in contrast, still offers the refined style of the 19th-century aristocracy. Once, empresses, archdukes and princesses met here to spend the winter and to enjoy the Atlantic setting; they stayed in luxurious hotels with stunning views of the Grande-Plage, the great beach, and they squandered immense fortunes on the green felt gaming tables of the Casino Bellevue. These days, those waves crash near vacationers engaging in more athletic forms of entertainment – the crowned heads of Europe have made way for those modern acrobats, the surfers. Biarritz has become the European capital of this sport. And there is another, equally important sport, that has conquered the Basques – golf. The lush green golf courses that extend in all directions would almost lead one to believe that golf has replaced pelota – a version of jay alai or handball – as the local sport. That's not quite true of course; every town and village boasts a pelota court, where the feverish game is played with a small fast ball made of sheepskin and fleece. The court usually stands beside the town hall and the parish church, with its distinctive engraved wooden galleries. Everywhere are white houses, decorated with sky blue paint, and with wooden beams painted bright green and red. The restaurants are charming; garish tablecloths are spread upon a great tables made of rough, dark wood. Huge fireplaces and bunches of red peppers adorn the walls; the peppers can be found in almost every Basque dish.

Solid respect for local traditions dictates the menu; a typical meal might call for *piperade* (scrambled eggs and ham), with such light wines as Ironléguy. Banquets and weddings are often enlivened with spectacular folk dances, to the joy of the tourists. The Basque language is still spoken; its roots have never been successfully traced, and no other languages are quite like it. Every French region along a border, after all, boasts greater idiosyncrasies than the other, inland regions; Corsica is perhaps the most extreme example of this rule, reinforced by its island nature.

Perhaps the most remarkable feature of Corsica is the rapidity with which one can shift from the snows of Cinto to the palm trees of Ajaccio, from the savage arena of Spelunca to the beautiful Gulf of Porto, from the cool forests of Vizzavona to the scorching desert of Agriates. The island boasts torrential streams, high mountain lakes, alpine meadows and dark chestnut groves, fragrant heather and towering pines, rocky inlets with bloody-red boulders and chalk cliffs rear 200 ft (60 m) above the waves. Some scholars say that Homer set a scene in the tenth book of the *Odyssey*, in which Ulysses combats mythical giants, in this natural harbor encircled by boulders. And the challenge of adventure is always available to those modern Ulysses who wish to explore the towns and inlets of this Island of Beauty. And so are Saint-Malo, Reims, Poitiers, Honfleur, Nancy, Dinan, Carcassonne, Orléans… and so many other places that *la douce France* can be considered an infinite resource.

A perfect hexagon

The natural plenty of the French soil is an integral part of our image of France, and paintings spread this image, transfigured in *en plein air* by Monet, precise and neat in *pointillisme* by Seurat, or reinvented by Van Gogh's visionary soul. But impressionist talent has been perhaps more faithful to reality than the green, purple and blue reveal. The French countryside is always waiting for acute observers to depict its landscape.

The hexagonal shape of France almost seems to have been planned at a drawing board, in the most logical fashion possible. The country is perfectly symmetrical – three continental and three maritime "facets"; one facet washed by the Atlantic, one by the Mediterranean and the last on the English Channel. In the middle is the Massif Central. From the steep gorges of the Verdon, with vertical drops of 2000 ft (610 m), to the volcanic cones of Auvergne, from the high Norman cliffs of Dieppe, wet with the foam of the crashing rollers of the Channel, to the sun-kissed beaches of the Côte d'Azur, the visitor can explore an incessantly changing landscape; few can claim to know this country well.

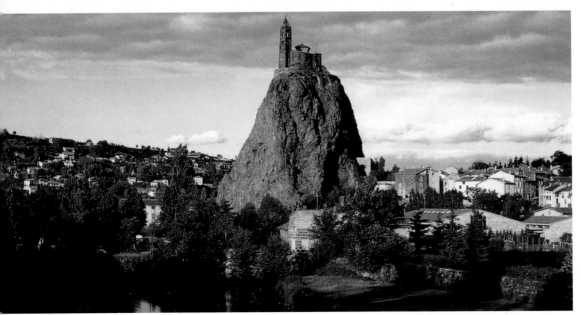

28 top *The Monts du Morvan have been protected by the creation in 1970 of a regional wildlife park. Set in the heart of Burgundy, the area is dotted with lakes which glitter in the forested landscape.*

28 bottom *The Auvergne is a region of outstanding beauty, a lake district with a splendid landscape. This view of a dramatic boulder crowned by a medieval abbey is not unique in this area.*

29 *The luxuriant Dordogne Valley boasts the splendid Château of Beynac, built in medieval times. Here, landscapes are still unspoiled; rivers wend their way across the landscape, and at each curve of the stream one sees a château or a church, like so many stone sentinels.*

Country landscapes

30 *The château of Jumilhac looms over the surrounding valley, its typical military architecture adorned by handsome corner turrets and slate roofs.*

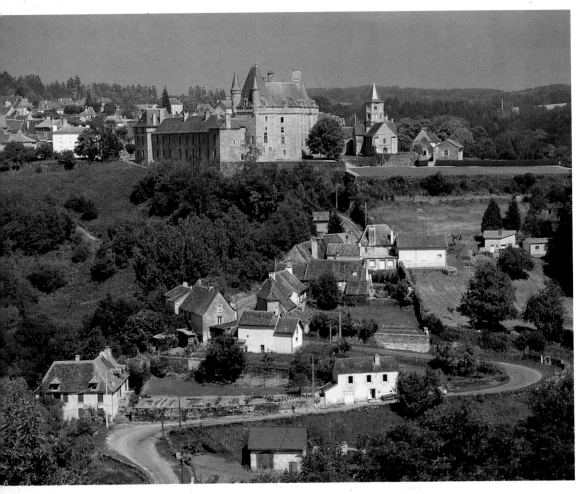

Haute-Provence presents sunny and winding landscapes with wooded hills and rock spurs emerging from a uniform, green plain where history has left memories of ancient civilizations in the many Roman sites and in strongholds like Jumilhac. This area claims primacy for the production of lavender, which permeates the air with its fragrance, together with the aromas of thyme and other herbs growing wild on the side of the nearby mountains. The enterprising citizens of Digne have dedicated an annual event to the "market" of lavender, from August to September, when the mistral blows through the valleys and takes everything apart. Provence is the region that has the widest variety of landscapes, as its northern limits are snow-capped calcareous mountains, and the southern ones the sandy beaches on the Mediterranean. Although it appears to be a contradiction, inland and coastal areas share a common characteristic – a brightness which has fans worldwide and which makes the region one of the main destinations for tourists. Nearly all modern artistic trends have been influenced by this brightness, particularly by the works of Cézanne, Picasso, Matisse, Signac, Monet, Van Gogh, and Le Corbusier.

31 *Solemn and imposing, an alpine range stands high above the bright landscape of Haute-Provence. Tilled fields alternate with somber scrublands, and here and there stands a small village, dotted with quaint pointed roofs, set on a gentle slope in a serene setting.*

Wine-growing regions

The French landscape is never dull – and the products of that landscape are as varied and surprising as the landscape itself. The visitor can sample a seemingly infinite range of wines, savoring the craft of the vintner, yet clearly detecting the original, pristine qualities of the fruit. Sparkling and refined Champagne – from the region of the same name – the full-bodied red wines of Burgundy, the well known Côte-du-Rhône and the agreeable white wines of Alsace, the universe of French wines offers something for every palate. The masters of this precious nectar devote endless care and attention to its creation; French wine rightly claims a place of honor in the cultural and artistic heritage of each region. These trellised vines bear witness to the effort and devotion lavished to maintain a pleasing order in terrace and hillside; that devotion pays off in the finished product. And tourists can sample that product in a tour of the vineyards and vintners, open to the public.

34-35 *Champagne is grown in three* départements. *Most of the grapes (80 percent) grown here are used in making Champagne.*

Brittany

The Breton region abounds in things to see and places to go; visitors are enthralled by the artistic and natural treasures, as well as by the intriguing character of the Bretons. The inhabitants' distinctive personality is perhaps a result of daily exposure to the rage and exuberance of the Atlantic Ocean; the elements have endowed the Bretons with a spirit of tenacity and determination. In the Bretons, strong religious faith combines with the stout Celtic soul; the result of this unusual alchemy is a popular imagination capable of concocting surreal and fantastic legends and myth. Thus, this region is the homeland of the Holy Grail and of Tristan and Isolde, whose story inspired Wagner's opera. The visitor can indulge in romantic reveries on the "actual" site of the legendary events. It is, in fact, possible to follow a route – parallel to tours of actual historical sites – of legendary sites featuring the heroes and characters of Arthurian legend. This is the land of sorcerer Merlin and of Lancelot du Lac, as much as it is the land of the megalithic monuments of Carnac and Menec, or the unsettling carved stone calvaries which date from the Middle Ages.

36-37 Small harbors crowded with boats, fishermen's watering holes with signs corroded by salt air, castles girt by ramparts and surrounded by close-pressed homes – these are just a few aspects of ordinary Breton life.

To live by the breath of the tide

38 top *The Church of Guimiliau in Brittany. In many Breton villages, artists and craftsmen have found concrete expression for the religious feelings of the inhabitants through* calvaires, *abounding in real and allegorical characters, displayed in the* enclos paroissiaux *or in countless churches and chapels.*

38 bottom *Wind and sea savage the jagged shoreline of a bay that has earned for itself the unsettling name of "Baie des Trépassés," or "Bay of the Dead."*

39 top *This home in the seaside resort of Quiberon is set on the far tip of the peninsula. The slow work of time and the ocean has linked this strip of granite to the mainland; Quiberon is now a major tourist attraction.*

39 bottom *The coastline of the peninsula of Quiberon is also called "Côte Sauvage," because of its harsh and daunting appearance.*

Living in time with the ocean

The photographs on these two pages show everyday life in Honfleur; this is just one of the many facets of life in Normandy. For the region is also a vast farmland, dotted with small neat fields, dairy farms and endless rows of apple trees, which yield the excellent local cider. Normandy also abounds in venerable abbeys, châteaux and manors, often described by Gustave Flaubert and Guy de Maupassant.

42-43 Mont-Saint-Michel is unlike anything else on earth. Set amid an expanse of ever-changing sands which are illuminated by the restless coastal light and flooded at regular intervals by the most powerful tides in Europe, the island-abbey rears up, a startling metaphor for medieval society.

44-45 Those who first see Normandy from the sea are astonished at the white expanse of the cliffs of Étretat; this huge geological formation is mirrored in the cobalt waters in an endless series of reflections.

46-47 This is a nighttime view of the old port of La Rochelle; among the town's many towers, the Tour de la Chaine, as its name suggests of closing the port with a great chain, at night and in times of danger.

Where space expands
in silence and solitude

48   *The region of Queyras abounds in attractions, both in winter and summer; the Guil valley is especially interesting, and lies in the shadow of Monviso, the summit of which is in Italy.*

49   *The French Alps attract millions of visitors who want to enjoy the unforgettable landscapes and relax mind and body with healthy sporting activities. From Briançon, the visitor*

can enjoy a wide variety of activities; the Parc National des Écrins, seen, here, is close by.

50-51   *The border between France and Italy crosses the snow-covered peak of Mont Blanc; each year, groups of intrepid mountain climbers reach the summit. This feat, first accomplished in 1786, requires great experience and the assistance of a guide.*

At the foot of the highest mountain in the Alps, Mont Blanc, lies the town of Chamonix; the vast glacier of Bossons separates the village from the peak, which glitters with thousands of crystal facets. As in so many other Alpine stations, an ancient village lies at the heart of Chamonix; around it, modern sport facilities, hotels, swimming pools, and restaurants have sprung up, and are now patronized by a sophisticated international clientele. The 7.25-mile (11.5-km) tunnel linking Chamonix and Courmayeur was reopened to traffic in 2002 following the terrible fire that devastated it in 1999. For those who prefer to sway in high winds at great height, a funicular connects the town to Entrèves – also on the Italian side – the cables pass over snowfields and glaciers, all the way up to Helbronner Point. From there, there is a gentle descent to the Val d'Aosta; passengers can enjoy breathtaking panoramas and dizzying views of sheer drops. The ski slopes of Chamonix swarm with an army of skiers, attracted by the pure air and the amazing views. At some distance from the bustling heart of the town, one can still find small chapels, ancient chalets, and – in the springtime – fields full of wildflowers, shrouded in a profound, all-enveloping silence.

54-55 *The Pyrenees extend from the Atlantic Ocean to the Mediterranean Sea. Their valleys descend northward, creating a number of mountainous realms. These narrow lands are linked by high passes, whose names – and steepness – are well known to the competitors of the Tour de France cycle race.*

The Mediterranean coast

56 and 56-57 *"Nice, the Beautiful"
truly deserves such a seductive nickname:
here, among modern condominiums
of debatable impact, iconic hotels, and
ancient little lanes scented like the sea,
it is possible to breathe in a sophisticated,
electric, and nostalgic atmosphere
everywhere you go.*

58-59 *All the splendor of the
Mediterranean seems to want to slip
among the blinding rocks and gorges of the
Calanques, between Cassis and Marseille.*

The Mediterranean islands

In bygone eras, the Maures mountain chain extended into the Mediterranean; the Hyères Islands formed part of the chain, and then gradually broke off, over the eons. Porquerolles Islands, back then, was covered with luxuriant pine forests, eucalyptus trees, heather, and myrtle. Although the island was swept by brush fires in the 19th century, and its vegetation was severely reduced, it still preserves a savage beauty.

Corsica

Corsica was occupied, in turn, by the Iberians, the Ligurians, the Etruscans, the Carthaginians – all these people settled and fought here. Then came the Romans' turn; the Empire used the island as a place of banishment and, according to legend, the philosopher Seneca languished here for several years as a prisoner. The Byzantines were the next lords of the island, followed by Franks, Saracens and, most recently, the Genoese, under whom the island enjoyed five centuries of relative stability. The Genoese overlordship came to an end in 1789, when Corsica became French. It is separated into two *départements* – Haute-Corse and Corse-du-Sud, it now enjoys partial political independence.

64-65 The kingdom of light is found north of the Mouth of Bonifacio, along the Corsican coastline, where only the limestone distinguishes itself from the blue of the sky and sea.

66-67 The small town of Bonifacio, built on a cliff 200 feet above sea level, catches the last rays of evening sunlight.

The lessons of life

France is generally considered a land where people know how to live well. What is the secret of this enviable reputation? In fact, the country is changing as fast as any other, and transition threatens the French life style. Nonetheless, at the time of writing, the French are defending – with resounding success – their style and quality of life, so much a part of the country's identity.

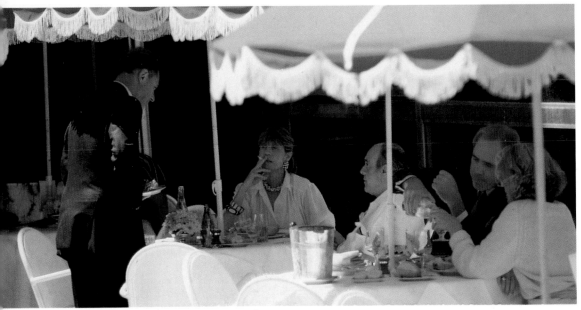

France is everywhere known as the country of *savoir vivre*, where a light nonchalance is exalted as a philosophy of life and where the secret of a happy life seems to have its origin, as reflected in the frequently cited *joie de vivre*. But what then is the formula that rewarded the french people with so many positive comments? Perhaps the quality of life is proportional to the human dimension, which everywhere degenerates too much in huge suburbs, chaotic highways and enormous factories. Paris is the only French metropolis and, together with the Île-de-France, includes almost one-fifth of the entire national population.
Urbanization, except for the capital, is not very advanced, so this country continues to be represented by regions marked by various and rich cultures reflecting local customs. Based on these presuppositions of equilibrium, France will go on avoiding standardization and will continue to export important things … haute couture, haute cuisine … remaining a symbol of refinement.

68 *A chat and a bite at a local café seems to be a fundamental ingredient of a Parisian day. The tables are set outdoors in the summer, behind glass in the winter.*

69 *One of the most attractive characteristics of the Parisian* savoir-faire, *and more generally the French one, is a knowledgeable disinterest in frills and decorative excess, a noble simplicity that characterizes, for example, this spartan Parisian Salon de Thé and the lady bystander.*

Parisian charm

The café is a fundamental feature of Parisian life. Oddly, the first café was not founded by a Frenchman, but by a Sicilian, a certain Procopio dei Costelli, who gave a French version of his name to his establishment – Le Procope. Located in Rue de l'Ancienne-Comédie, this café soon became the meeting place for Parisian artists. Literary and political generations followed one after the others – Voltaire, d'Alambert and Diderot, and then the Romantics, lastly Gambetta and his journalist friends. Toward the end of the last century, the café became, once again, an exquisitely literary realm, with Paul Verlaine and company.

72-73 The terrace of the Restaurant Grande Cascade, in the Bois de Boulogne.

74 and 75　*It is common knowledge that everything in the world of haute couture converges in Paris, where half the planet and the entire universe of high fashion are represented by "ambassadors" like the house of Nina Ricci (left) or Karl Lagerfeld (right, accompanied by his mannequins). Here, before the eyes of an audience of intellectuals, artists, and aristocrats, the superfluous becomes an important opportunity for meetings and high-society networking, in addition to, of course, a significant source of business.*

Legends à la carte

French cuisine is world renowned, both for its quality and for the variety of dishes. Here food is an art, a philosophy, even a religion, with great chefs as high priests and fine restaurants as temples in which the ritual secrets are jealously preserved. Classic French cuisine requires time and devotion to detail, along with such fresh and delicate ingredients as truffles, mushrooms, cognac, butter,

78-79 Cognac is distilled – and redistilled – from wine made from "folle-blanche" grapes; the distilling process follows methods and uses equipment that date back over the centuries. This picture perfectly depicts the patient labor of the distillers who make cognac, amidst hundreds of oaken barrels. A candle is used to warm the liquid prior to tasting.

and cream. Herbs and spices are skillfully blended into exquisite sauces. Nouvelle cuisine, long fashionable, calls for a simpler approach to sauces and condiments, and emphasizes the natural flavors of the ingredients. Local cuisines are also greatly prized. The construction of Paris' great boulevards engendered the establishment of the city's famous restaurants, and in them one can often see original décor from that period. At the Tour d'Argent, one can sit by large windows and look out at the apse of Notre-Dame; at Le Grand Véfour, one can sit where Napoleon Bonaparte or Jean Cocteau once dined.

Ancient traditions

80-81 *Around the world, late summer is harvest time. But for farmers in the Deux-Sèvres area, machinery has not entirely replaced the traditional methods.*

At La Garette and at Coulon, visitors can rent a boat to tour the Parc Naturel du Marais Poitevin, one of the largest in France, extended over 150,000 acres (60,000 hectares) in area. There are two types of "marais" – the wetlands variety, extending from Niort to Damvix (37,000 acres/15,000 hectares), which has been dubbed the "Green Venice," with an intricate network of channels running under a canopy of poplars and beeches. This sort of "marais" is devoted to horticulture, and one can only get around by boat. There is another kind, the "dry marais" (98,800 acres/40,000 hectares); this "marais" is also crisscrossed by drainage canals, but cattle are grazed here.

Oysters, a delicacy from the sea

Oysters are fished heavily off the Channel and Atlantic coasts. In the Gulf of Morbihan, especially, oysters are caught in the following manner: baby oysters (they are usually 1/3 mm in size) which float with the currents attach themselves to the nets set out for this purpose. After eight months, the oysters are removed and placed in oyster farms. After two or three years, when they have attained the right size, they are removed and shipped to special oyster plants where another year goes by before they are ready to eat.

Dance and costume

In France, each region possesses a traditional costume. Of course, the costumes are rarely worn nowadays, but they are shown off with pride during festivals. The most remarkable costumes are those of Alsace, Brittany – with lovely lace headgear – and the Pays Basque. The costumes of Arles are described at length in the works of Alphonse Daudet and Frédéric Mistral.

Passion on horseback

The *gardians* of the Camargue have become legendary for their skill in breaking wild horses and fierce bulls. In this land, among ponds and marshes, white horses live practically wild, alongside black bulls that are dangerous to approach – ever ready to charge at careless tourists. Great care is required to transport these animals to the *corridas* in Arles or Nîmes, where they are sacrificed to the applause of the public, who are seated on the stone steps of ancient Roman arenas. Lassoed and haltered, their horns padded to protect them during transport, the bulls are loaded onto special vehicles. Transporting them is no less complicated; they are a source of considerable concern to the *gardians* because they are quite agile, and sometimes leap over the sides of the arena, causing the spectators to scatter. Aside from bullfights, the Provençals are fond of other forms of sport with bulls, often less bloody. In the famed *course à la cocarde*, for instance, young men snatch a ribbon pinned between the horns of the bull.

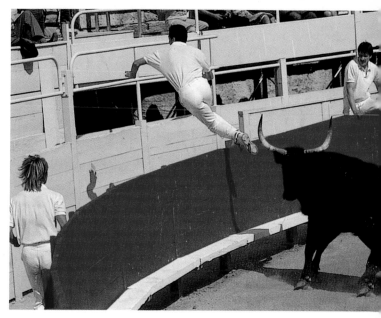

In search of history

Each part of France boasts architectural treasures, whether they be Romanesque churches, Gothic cathedrals or châteaux dating from the Renaissance or later; there are fortified towns and entire neighborhoods that have preserved the same appearance for centuries.

In France, each historical stage is displayed with an abundance of temples, palaces, castles and cathedrals, in a millenarian carousel involving the capital as well as the farthest province. The driving force of such vast initiative is certainly due to the richness of open and cultivated minds, but also – and above all else – to the "grandeur" which has promoted titanic achievements for nationalistic conceit and a desire for eternity. Time has never stopped; rather, it appears to have chosen committing challenge to anticipate the aesthetic/architectural dictates of the coming century. The near future has been already overlapped by the inspiration of a Défense district on the Paris outskirts, by the holiday center "La Grande Motte" on the Languedoc coast, or by the Centre Pompidou. In France, perhaps, someone is already designing the 22nd century.

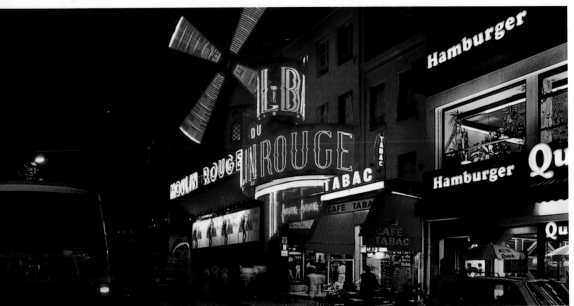

90 top *The great avenue of the Champs-Elysées intersects with the Place de l'Etoile, where twelve main streets lead away from the monumental Arc de Triomphe.*

90 bottom *The Moulin Rouge and Place Pigalle have been the regular meetinig places of Paris's nightowls for many generations.*

91 *The Eiffel Tower, now over a century old, was completed in 1889. It is more than 900 ft (274 m) in height.*

The city
of light

92 left *The white cupola of Sacré-Coeur, a basilica that surveys all of Paris from atop Montmartre. From the lantern, visitors can enjoy a splendid panorama.*

92 right *Le Café des Deux Magots, in Saint-Germain-des-Prés, became famous in the Fifties when it was chosen as a favorite meeting place by the French Existentialists. It has always been a popular Parisian rendezvous.*

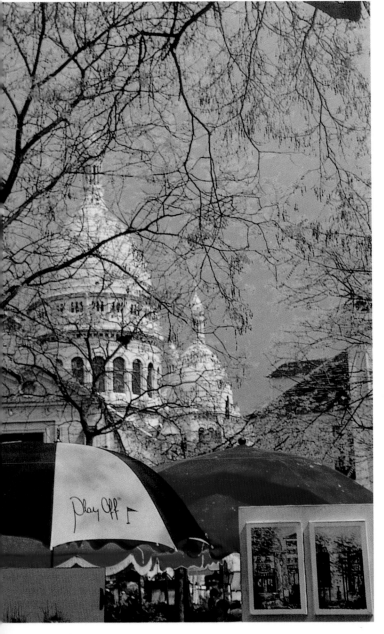

93 *Not far from the Opéra, in the 9h arrondissement, is the Galeries Lafayette, a world-famous Parisian department store.*

94-95 *A singular view of Île de la Cité, with a close-up of Notre-Dame cathedral and its renowned spire.*

95 top *From the top of Notre-Dame, a thoughtful gargoyle in the form of a demon seems saddened under the autumnal Paris sky. The use of these elements, whether functional (as the end of a drainpipe) or decorative (as in this case), reached its climax at the height of the construction of Paris' majestic cathedral, in the 13th century, when the towers on the façade were completed (1245).*

95 bottom *All the energy of Paris converges in the majestic boulevard of the Champs-Elysées, just over one mile of thoroughfare through luxury and history, leading from the Arc de Triomphe to Place de la Concorde, seen in the background. The first tree-lined avenue, then in the middle of fields, was opened in 1616 on the orders of Maria de' Medici.*

96 and 97 *The Louvre is so big, and the collections it holds so important, it diminishes the presence of humans; it is easy for visitors to feel insignificant in the presence of so much history and wealth. To balance the austerity of the overall setting, offset in part by the charming atmosphere of Paris, the steel and glass pyramid by I.M. Pei was added in 1988.*

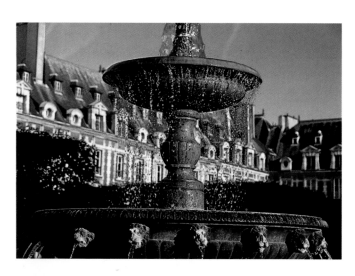

98 top *One of the four fountains in Place des Vosges stands out against a background of 17th-century buildings, whose stylistic unity makes this spot in Paris truly incomparable. As known by many, this was the first monumental square in the city.*

98 bottom *The sharp face of Charles Garnier is immortalized in bronze in front of the Opéra of Paris. The young architect, creator of this temple of opera, symphonic music, and dance, dedicated a good part of his life to the work and hit the style on the mark: his masterpiece is probably the building most representative of the Napoleon IIIrd style.*

98-99 *The northwesternmost point on the Île de la Cité, Pont Neuf extends its mighty sturdiness across the waters of the Seine. Despite its name, it is the oldest bridge still in existence in Paris. Its construction was ordered by Henry III, in the last quarter of the 16th century.*

99 top *The most romantic of romantic rides seems to be that along the Seine aboard the highly famous bâteaux-mouches (meaning "fly-boats" – as in the insect –, agile, light, and able to load a large number of passengers). It is almost, at least for tourists, a Parisian institution, but their origin can be found in the Mouche quarter in Lyon, where the first of their kind were made, and maybe also in the fact that they were used for espionage purposes (from the word* mouchard, *meaning "spy").*

100-101 and 101 top It is not uncommon for a very innovative architectural creation to leave the public unhappy, but it happens quite often that, with time, that same creation can become an inexorable part of the urban landscape. This is the case with the Georges Pompidou Centre National d'Art et de Culture, inaugurated in 1977 and since become one of the most popular and important cultural centers in the world.

101 center left In the square in front of the Pompidou Center, the ultra-imaginative birds by Jean Tinguely and Niki de Saint-Phalle adorn the Fontaine Beaubourg (1980), another work so "out of place" as to become irreplaceable.

101 center right and bottom When it comes to modernity, the neighborhood of La Défense has established an even higher standard for similar zones in other cities with an eye on the future. The origin of the plan for this area dates back to 1958, but the various structures were completed in several phases, influenced by an equal number of tastes and styles and, above all, the economic conditions at the time. There are many shopping centers, residential buildings, hotels, and the offices of large corporations here, perfectly centered around the Grande Arche (bottom), inaugurated in 1989 as the outermost end of the Axe Historique, or the series of avenues that cross the capital as far as the Arc de Triomphe, to which the Arche constitutes a futuristic counterpoint.

Silk spinner to the king

Lyon is France's second-largest city. Built at the foot of a hill, at the confluence of the rivers Saône and Rhône, Lyon is often shrouded in heavy fog. The old section of the city is the most extensive complex of Renaissance and 15th-century monuments to be found in France. Nothing could be more agreeable than a pleasant stroll through the Vieux-Lyon district, followed by a meal in a *bouchon*, one of Lyon's typical restaurants. Lyon first became an industrial center in the 16th century, with the manufacture of silk. Francis I was concerned by France's volume of imported silk, and so he founded a royal manufactory, and hired expert spinners from Genoa.

Historic towns

104 top *The city of Nancy is best known for the spectacular Place Stanislas, a masterpiece of mid-18th-century architecture. The cast-iron gate, chased with gold, is the work of Jean Lamour; the fountains are by the sculptor Barthélémy Guibal.*

104 bottom *The cathedral of Notre-Dame, in the central Place du Cardinal Luçon, overlooks the city of Reims. This Gothic masterpiece boasts majestic towers, over 270 feet tall; a rose window about 40 feet across in the western facade; and fine statues that adorn the portals.*

105 *In the heart of the old section of Rouen, where automobiles are forbidden, pedestrians walk under the Gros-Horloge, an arch with a giant clock dial on both sides. The clockworks date from 1389.*

106-107 *At the confluence of the Ille and the Rhine, and crisscrossed by the canals that connect the two rivers, Strasbourg lives at two radically different speeds. The city is at once a major European metropolis and a venerable and charming Alsatian provincial town.*

108-109 *Since 1864, the basilica of Notre Dame de la Garde has watched over Marseille and its Vieux Port, since time immemorial the fulcrum of business and activity in this seaside city of many faces, once not all reassuring. At the beginning of a new century, Marseille is at the center of the magnificent Euroméditerranée development project, which intends to make it the greatest port in the Mediterranean.*

The deathless relics of Roman civilization

110 top *The Roman amphitheater in Orange; the wall behind the stage is still intact.*

110 bottom *The bridge at Avignon, built in the 12th century.*

110-111 *The Roman amphitheater at Arles, built in the 1st century A.D., was used as a fortress in the Middle Ages; hence the three watchtowers.*

112-113 *The fortified medieval village of Aigues-Mortes lies just west of the Camargue.*

In the heart of Languedoc

An ancient Roman fortress, built on the foothills of the Pyrenees, Carcassonne was expanded by the Visigoths. After the Franks took over, the town continued to grow until the 13th century, when it was completely surrounded by walls. The River Aude separates the Ville Basse, or "low town," from the Cité, or city center, with the most remarkable set of medieval walls in Europe. The entire complex is in a perfect state of conservation, largely due to the complete restoration performed in the 19th century by the architect Eugène Emmanuel Viollet-le-Duc (1814-79).

116-117 A visit to the abbey of Sénanque is one of the most thrilling that can be imagined, especially in May when the fields of lavender are ready to be harvested and give off an intoxicating scent. This is a place out of the Middle Ages that has been preserved in a lonely valley in the Vaucluse, in Provence, where, in 1148, the Cistercians founded a complex whose simple harmony inspires a timeless sense of purity and genuine spirituality.

A prayer in stone and glass

Work began on Chartres Cathedral in 1194. This church offered a second birth to Gothic architecture. The building is remarkably homogeneous, chiefly because its construction spanned no more than three decades; it served as a classic model for the cathedrals built in later years in Reims and Amiens. The choir of Chartres, larger than any other, and the immense transept, designed to accommodate vast throngs, seem to have been built in order to allow the pilgrims to gather as close as possible to the holy altar. This is a building of the people, in which burghers, peasants and craftsmen vied with princes in their generosity, devotion and in the honor of placing their coat of arms or that of their guild in the stained glass, in eternal commemoration.

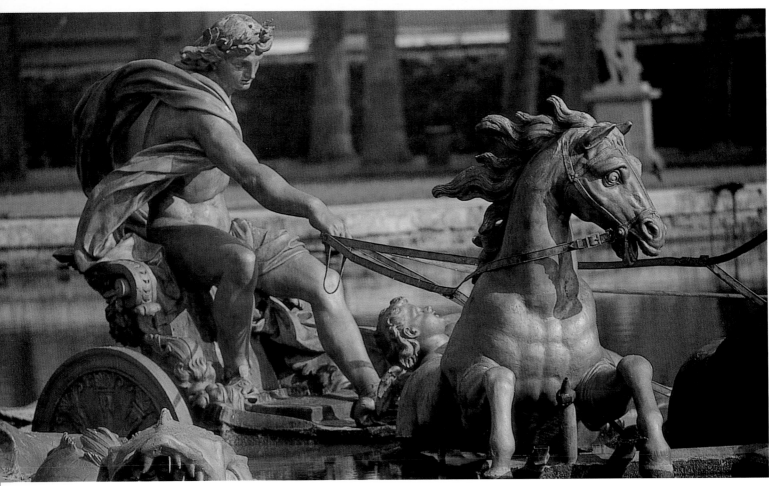

The Palace of the Sun King

When Louis XIV took the throne, nothing more than a hunting lodge stood where Versailles now stands. The king quickly decided that the lodge needed some changes. He "stole" the team of architects and artists that his finance minister, Nicolas Fouquet, had employed to build Vaux-le-Vicomte, and ordered them to embellish and expand on the existing structure. Le Brun was in charge of the buildings, while Le Nôtre oversaw the planning and decoration of the gardens. Work went on unceasingly, as Louis XIV became increasingly ambitious, and kept adding buildings. At last, in 1682, the king and his court took up residence in Versailles, while work was still proceeding: the architect Jules Hardouin Mansart still had 36,000 soldiers and laborers on the job. Versailles is now a legend that bears witness to the remarkable vigor of French art in the 17th and 18th centuries.

A journey through the Renaissance

122-123 Water is queen of the gardens at the château of Fontainbleau, whose parterre was the work of the famous landscape architect André Le Nôtre, who added prestige to almost all the royal and noble French residences of the mid-17th century. He was the one to create the French-style garden still desired today by those who can afford it. The castle, built by Francis I (1494-1515), takes its name from the Fontaine Belle-Eau, the "Fountain of the Beautiful Water," a spring that was probably located where the English garden of the castle (1812) now stands. This complex building, containing countless rooms and lavish decorative details, was of course witness to several more or less important historical events, but the most famous and the most moving was the first abdication of Napoleon Bonaparte, France's fearsome emperor. He signed his renunciation of the throne of France and Italy here in July 1814, and made his famous "farewell" to the Old Guard, saluting the finest of his troops.

124 top *The château of Azay-le-Rideau was built on the River Indre. The corner turrets, reflected in the river, are built in the graceful style of the early French Renaissance.*

124 bottom *The château of Moulin was built near Lassay, for Philippe du Moulin. It is made up of two buildings, mirrored in the waters of the moat.*

124-125 *The château of Chambord stands on the left bank of the Loire. Set within an enclosure, it possesses a central keep with four towers. Its distinguishing feature is the contrast between the simplicity of its façade and the welter of adornments upon the keep.*

126-127 *The château of Amboise, in the town where Leonardo da Vinci died in 1519, is built on a rock overlooking the Loire. It stands between two enormous round towers; the Tour des Minimes, near the Loire, could be reached on horseback due to a spiral ramp.*

128 *The solitary abbey, village and fortress of Mont-Saint-Michel is one of the most surprising spots in the whole of France and rises out of the bay of the same name in the Gulf of Saint-Malo.*